More Money Less Hussle.
Money Made Easy Opportunities while You Work Less.

James .S. Smith

Table of content

Chapter 1

More Money Less Hassle: How To Bill Your
Clients Better

To ensure the success of your business,
billing is a crucial process that should not be
overlooked. Unfortunately, many
entrepreneurs prioritize the actual work
over getting paid for it, resulting in
inefficiency. However, for a profitable
business, streamlining and optimizing the
billing process should be a top priority. By
following the tips provided, you can simplify
your billing process, receive payments
faster, and reduce invoice-related
headaches.

One effective strategy is to offer an early
payment discount to incentivize clients to
pay before the due date. This is especially
important for North American businesses,
as cash flow is often a major challenge. By
providing a credit of X% for each invoice
paid ahead of schedule, you can maintain a
more consistent cash flow. It is important to

offer credit rather than a plain discount, as this ensures that the client fulfills their end of the agreement before receiving the benefit.

Encouraging clients to opt for monthly retainers instead of project-based work can also contribute to a more stable cash flow. Retainers guarantee a regular income and reduce the time spent searching for new projects. Additionally, retainers benefit clients by prioritizing their work and allowing for a deeper understanding of their needs.

Requiring up-front payments can be a smart business move to address the issue of non-payment. By collecting payment in advance, you eliminate the risk of unpaid work and ensure the client's commitment to the project. This approach helps to avoid frustrating situations where clients become unresponsive after initially expressing interest.

Automating payment reminders is a polite and effective way to prompt clients to submit overdue payments. Just like other service providers, sending reminders at regular intervals after missed payments is good business practice.

If managing accounts receivable proves to be a challenge for you, consider hiring an online bookkeeper. Ignite Spot, for example, specializes in streamlining financial processes and can take on the responsibility of managing accounts receivable for your business. By outsourcing this task, you can focus on what you do best while ensuring that your finances are in order.

By implementing these strategies, you can improve your billing process, increase your income, and reduce unnecessary stress. Remember, effective billing is key to the success and longevity of your business.

Chapter 2

More Money Less Hustle:The Secret to Making More Money While Doing Less.

1. Optimize Your Productivity: At IWT, we frequently discuss the importance of investing. Savvy investors understand the immense benefits of starting early and investing as much as possible. The same concept applies to your work. During your twenties and thirties, when ambition, drive, and energy are at their peak, it is crucial to front-load your efforts. By dedicating weekends, late nights, and extra hours to your work in the early stages of your career or business, you will pave the way for a future where you can work less and earn more. The impact of your current efforts will compound over time. As the saying goes, "The best time to plant a tree was 20 years ago. The second best time is today." Seize the opportunity while you still have the energy and drive, and you will reap the rewards in the long run. While immediate

results may not be evident, a powerful shift will gradually occur.

2. Diversify Your Income Sources: If your goal is to work fewer hours and increase your income, it is crucial to develop multiple streams of income. You might wonder if this means more work rather than less (especially in the beginning, as mentioned in point #1). However, the purpose of multiple income streams is to reduce your reliance on a single

source. Consider this scenario: Your boss informs you that you will need to work additional hours on a challenging project next quarter. Naturally, you anticipate a raise or promotion to accompany the increased workload. Unfortunately, your assumptions are incorrect. Not only will you be working longer hours, but your salary will remain the same (which is already inadequate). Without alternative income streams, you will find yourself trapped. Responsibilities such as rent, mortgage payments, and dependents, coupled with student loans and credit card debt, leave you with no choice but to stay in your current job. Now, envision a different situation: Your boss is aware that you have been working on a side hustle for several years, and it has been thriving. Your side income is nearly equivalent to your regular job's earnings. When your boss assigns you additional tasks, you immediately request a raise to compensate for the increased workload. You are in a win-win situation. If your request is denied, you can quit because your side income is sufficient to sustain you until you secure a new job or transition to full-time with your side hustle. If your request is granted, fantastic! You have just obtained a raise, allowing you to earn more while working fewer hours after the project's completion. By incorporating various income sources like side hustles, passive income, residual income, or interest from investments, you gain control over your financial future rather than relying on others.

3. Streamline Your Finances: One of the most effective methods for achieving a work-life balance with increased income is to let your money work for you. Automating your finances is an invaluable investment of time and effort as you strive to work less and earn more. By automating your financial transactions, you enable your money to work harder. Set up automatic withdrawals from your paycheck, directing funds into a Roth IRA or stock investments. Define a fixed monthly amount and allow your bank or a finance app to handle the process seamlessly. This way, you won't even have to think about it. By automating your finances, you create a system that supports your financial goals without requiring constant attention and effort.

Chapter 3

Achieving Wealth Without Endless Hustle:
Unlocking Financial Success.

Growing up, I experienced a unique family
dynamic that shaped my perspective on
money. As a young, single mother, my mom
worked tirelessly to make ends meet with
two jobs. Financially, it was challenging for
her to support me on her own, so we lived
with my hardworking grandparents until I
was old enough to attend college. Hailing
from the Midwest, my grandparents were
blue-collar individuals who epitomized the
values of hard work and self-reliance.
However, their unintentional teachings
about money unknowingly instilled some
toxic beliefs within me, leading to financial
turmoil later in life.

One of the toxic money beliefs I acquired
was the notion that to earn a good living, I
had to sacrifice time with loved ones. I
witnessed my grandfather frequently absent
from home for long periods due to his work

as a truck driver. The limited time he spent with our family taught me that success required sacrificing personal relationships a detrimental belief that hindered my financial journey.

Similarly, my grandmother, even though working from home, devoted countless hours to her. Running a home daycare during the day and sewing pool skimmer nets in the evenings, she exemplified the belief that only through working relentlessly could financial progress be achieved. This toxic money belief further reinforced the idea that success necessitated tirelessly working long hours.

Furthermore, my grandparents' approach to tasks and projects contributed to a third toxic money belief. They never sought external help, opting to tackle every challenge themselves. Whether it was fixing a sink, repairing a car, or creating a costume, they believed it was wasteful to pay others for assistance. Consequently, I grew up believing that relying on others for help was irresponsible and that I had to become self-sufficient in all aspects of life.

Carrying these toxic money beliefs into adulthood, I found myself immersed in a culture that glorifies constant work and sacrifice. While studying at college, I juggled multiple jobs, yet financial stability remained elusive. Even in my free time, I would engage in activities such as detailing my car or making my scarves, fearing the judgment of my grandparents if I paid someone else for these services.

Upon entering the workforce, I still encountered the same workaholic mindset. Operating on an on-call basis, my schedule was unpredictable, hindering my ability to enjoy a fulfilling social life. This sacrifice was deemed necessary as I had witnessed my grandfather's absence throughout my hustle-and-grind childhood. However, this constant grind eventually led to burnout and resentment toward my earned job beyond the confines of a demanding work schedule.

Hence, I decided to venture into entrepreneurship and establish my counseling practice, convinced that this path would grant me both wealth and freedom. I envisioned working fewer hours while reaping substantial financial rewards, inspired by the success stories of other entrepreneurs. Enthusiastically, I invested a significant amount of money into my new business, anticipating rapid growth and a comfortable income.

Unfortunately, building a profitable business proved to be more challenging than I had anticipated. Despite putting in the same hours as before, I faced the daunting reality of forgoing a stable paycheck and benefits. The expected influx of money did not materialize, leaving me overwhelmed with bills and financial anxiety.

Struggling to navigate this money drama, I questioned how to keep my business afloat while simultaneously supporting myself. Sleepless nights were spent brainstorming ways to generate more income at a rapid pace, desperately seeking a solution.

In conclusion, my journey toward financial success was marred by toxic money beliefs inherited from my family. The arduous hustle and grind culture I grew up with, combined with unrealistic expectations of entrepreneurship, created a disheartening cycle of financial instability. However, by acknowledging and challenging these toxic beliefs, it is possible to reframe our approach to money and achieve wealth without sacrificing our well-being.

Chapter 4

More Money Less Hustle:Increasing Income and Minimizing Stress:

1. Seek Emotional Support: Instead of bottling up your financial problems, consider talking to someone you trust. Sharing your concerns and fears can provide stress relief and help put things into perspective. It doesn't matter if the person you confide in can solve your problems; their willingness to listen without judgment can make a difference. Additionally, professional advice from organizations that offer free counseling on financial matters can be valuable.

2. Involve Your Family: Financial issues can impact the entire family, so it's important to keep them informed and seek their support. Let them express their concerns and offer suggestions for resolving the problems. Engaging in low-cost or free family activities can also help relieve stress and maintain a positive atmosphere.

3. Assess Your Finances: Ignoring bills and statements will only worsen your situation. Take stock of your income, debt, and spending by tracking your finances for at least a month. Websites and apps can assist you in this process, or you can gather receipts and review bank and credit card statements. This detailed overview will provide a clearer understanding of your financial standing and allow you to regain control.

4. Include All Sources of Income: In addition to your salary, consider bonuses, benefits, alimony, child support, and interest received as part of your income.

5. Track All Expenses: Even seemingly small expenses can add up over time, so keep a record of everything you spend. This will help you identify spending patterns and develop a budget to address your financial problems.

6. List Your Debts: Make sure to include past-due bills, late fees, and minimum

payments, as well as any outstanding debts owed to family or friends.

7. Identify Triggers and Patterns: Recognize what prompts you to spend money impulsively, such as boredom or stress. Understanding these triggers can help you find alternative ways to cope without damaging your finances.

By following these tips, you can work towards increasing your income and reducing financial stress professionally and proactively.

Chapter 5

Money Made Easy: A Professional Approach to Financial Management

In today's fast-paced world, money plays a crucial role in our lives. It affords us not only the necessities but also the luxuries we desire. However, managing our finances can often seem overwhelming and complex. That is why it is essential to adopt a professional approach to money management, making it easy to navigate the financial landscape and achieve our goals. In this article, we will explore some key strategies and tools that can help us make money management a breeze.

One of the first steps towards making money management easy is setting clear financial goals. Without a clear direction, it is easy to get lost in the maze of financial decisions. Whether it is saving for a dream vacation, purchasing a new home, or planning for retirement, defining our goals allows us to align our financial actions accordingly. By establishing specific, measurable, achievable, relevant, and time-bound (SMART) goals, we can create a roadmap toward financial success.

Budgeting is another crucial tool in our professional money management arsenal. Creating a budget helps in tracking our income and expenses, allowing us to identify areas where we can cut back or make adjustments. By allocating our resources effectively, we can avoid unnecessary debt and ensure that our spending aligns with our financial goals. Numerous online tools and mobile apps are available to assist in budgeting, making it easier than ever to stay on top of our finances.

Saving is an integral part of effective money management. It provides us with a safety net during emergencies and paves the way for future financial security. Developing a habit of saving, even if it is a small amount each month, can go a long way in building wealth over time. Automatic transfers from our checking account to a dedicated savings account can make this process effortless and ensure that we consistently set aside money for our future.

Investing is another avenue to grow our wealth and make money easy. While it may seem daunting at first, with the right knowledge and guidance, anyone can become a successful investor. Diversifying our investment portfolio, understanding risk tolerance, and staying informed about market trends are essential aspects of a professional approach to investing. Seeking advice from financial advisors can provide valuable insights and help us make informed decisions.

Debt management is a critical aspect of money made easy. High-interest debts can quickly snowball and become overwhelming, hindering our financial progress. Adopting a proactive approach to debt management, such as paying off high-interest debts first and negotiating for lower interest rates, can save us thousands of dollars in the long run. It is crucial to stay disciplined and avoid unnecessary debt to maintain a healthy financial position.

Finally, staying informed about personal finance and keeping up with the changing financial landscape is vital in our journey towards making money easy. Reading books, attending seminars, and following reputable financial blogs can provide valuable insights and tips for effective money management. The more knowledge we have, the better equipped we are to make informed financial decisions and secure our financial future.

In conclusion, adopting a professional approach to money management can make our financial journey easier and more successful. By setting clear goals, budgeting effectively, saving regularly, investing wisely, managing debt, and staying informed, we can navigate the financial landscape with confidence. While it may require some initial effort and discipline, the rewards of financial freedom and security are well worth it. So, let's make money easy by embracing a professional mindset toward managing our finances.

91 tips to make cool cash effortlessly and timely.

Whether you are a student looking to earn some extra cash, a stay-at-home parent seeking a flexible source of income, or simply someone interested in increasing your financial stability, here are 91 tips that will help you make cool cash with less effort :

1. Invest in stocks and bonds: Research and invest in stable companies or government bonds to earn passive income.

2. Start a blog: Share your knowledge and expertise on a topic you are passionate about and monetize it through ads or sponsored content.

3. Become a freelancer: Offer your skills and services on platforms like Upwork or Fiverr to earn money on your terms.

4. Rent out your space: If you have a spare room or property, consider renting it out through platforms like Airbnb.

5. Create and sell an online course: Share your expertise by creating a course and selling

it on platforms like Udemy or Teachable.

6. Become a virtual assistant: Offer administrative support to busy professionals remotely.

7. Invest in real estate: Consider purchasing properties to generate rental income.

8. Offer consulting services: Capitalize on your industry knowledge and provide consultation to businesses or individuals.

9. Start an e-commerce business: Create an online store and sell products that align with your interests or expertise.

10. Become a social media influencer: Grow yours following on platforms like Instagram or YouTube and partner with brands for sponsored posts.

11. Rent out your belongings: If you have equipment or items that are not in use, rent them out to others through platforms like Fat Llama.

12. Affiliate marketing: Promote products or services and earn a commission for each successful referral.

13. Participate in online surveys: Sign up for reputable survey websites to earn money for sharing your opinions.

14. Become a mystery shopper: Get paid to evaluate the quality of products and services by visiting stores anonymously.

15. Offer pet sitting services: Take care of pets when their owners are away and earn extra income.

16. Create and sell digital products: Design and sell digital products like templates, graphics, or ebooks.

17. Get paid for writing reviews: Share your thoughts on products or services and get paid for your valuable feedback.

18. Offer resume writing services: Help individuals create professional resumes and cover letters.

19. Become a transcriptionist: Convert audio or video recordings into written documents and get paid per task.

20. Start a YouTube channel: Create engaging video content and earn revenue through ads or brand partnerships.

21. Invest in peer-to-peer lending: Lend money to individuals or businesses and earn interest on your investment.

22. Offer meal planning services: Help individuals or families plan their meals efficiently and save money on groceries.

23. Rent out your car: If you have a car that you rarely use, consider renting it out through platforms like Turo.

24. Sell handmade crafts: If you have a creative hobby, turn it into a business by selling your crafts online.

25. Become a language tutor: Teach others a language you are fluent in and earn money per lesson.

26. Start a podcast: Share your knowledge or interests through podcasts and monetize them through sponsorships or donations.

27. Offer graphic design services: Create logos, banners, or illustrations for clients on a freelance basis.

28. Participate in focus groups: Share your opinions on new products or services and get paid for your time.

29. Become a tour guide: If you live in a tourist destination, offer guided tours and share your knowledge with visitors.

30. Invest in crowdfunding projects: Support innovative projects and earn returns on your investment.

31. Offer social media management services: Help businesses grow their online presence by managing their social media accounts.

32. Rent out your parking space: If you have a parking spot in a desirable location, rent it out to others who need it.

33. Become a proofreader: Offer your proofreading services to individuals or businesses to ensure error-free content.

34. Sell stock photos: If you have a passion for photography, sell your high-quality images to stock photo websites.

35. Offer online tutoring: Help students excel in their academics by offering online tutoring sessions.

36. Become an affiliate for online courses: Promote online courses and earn a commission for each successful referral.

37. Offer SEO services: Help businesses improve their search engine rankings and increase their online visibility.

38. Start a subscription box service: Curate and sell themed boxes of products to subscribers every month.

39. Invest in dividend-paying stocks: Choose stocks that regularly distribute dividends to earn passive income.

40. Offer event planning services: Help individuals or businesses organize and execute successful events.

41. Start a dropshipping business: Set up an online store and sell products without having to manage inventory.

42. Offer personalized coaching services: Help individuals achieve their personal or professional goals through coaching sessions.

43. Become a voice-over artist: If you have a good voice, offer your services for commercials, audiobooks, or animations.

44. Start an affiliate marketing blog: Create a blog focused on a specific niche and earn money through affiliate marketing.

45. Offer online fitness training: Help individuals achieve their fitness goals by offering personalized training and nutrition plans online.

46. Become a driver for ride-sharing services: Use your car to earn money by providing transportation services.

47. Offer online dating profile writing services: Help individuals create compelling profiles to attract potential partners.

48. Invest in index funds: Diversify your investment portfolio by investing in low-cost index funds.

49. Offer virtual event planning services: Help businesses organize and host virtual conferences or webinars.

50. Become a product reviewer: Get paid to test and review products and share your honest opinions.

51. Start a podcast editing service: Help podcasters edit and produce high-quality episodes.

52. Offer online language translation services: Translate written content or documents from one language to another.

53. Become a social media advertising specialist: Help businesses create and manage effective advertising campaigns on social media platforms.

54. Offer resume design services: Create visually appealing and professional resumes for individuals.

55. Invest in cryptocurrency: Educate yourself about cryptocurrencies and invest in promising projects.

56. Offer online music lessons: Teach others to play a musical instrument or improve their singing skills through virtual lessons.

57. Become a personal shopper: Offer your services to busy individuals who need assistance with shopping or gift selection.

58. Offer website design services: Create visually appealing and functional websites for individuals or businesses.

59. Start a niche affiliate marketing website: Build a website focused on a specific niche and earn money through affiliate marketing.

60. Become a life coach: Help individuals overcome obstacles and achieve personal or professional success.

61. Offer online yoga classes: Teach yoga classes through video conferencing platforms and earn money per class.

62. Invest in rental properties: Purchase properties and earn rental income from tenants.

63. Offer social media content creation services: Create engaging and shareable

content for businesses to use on their social media platforms.

64. Become a data entry specialist: Offer your services to businesses or individuals who need help entering data accurately and efficiently.

65. Offer website maintenance services: Help businesses keep their websites updated and secure.

66. Start an online travel agency: Offer travel planning services and earn commissions from bookings.

67. Become a freelance translator: Translate written content from one language to another on a freelance basis.

68. Offer online coaching for specific skills: Teach others skills such as coding, photography, or writing through virtual coaching sessions.

69. Become a ghostwriter: Write articles, blog posts, or books for individuals or businesses who require assistance.

70. Offer proofreading and editing services: Help individuals or businesses polish their written content before publication.

71. Invest in dividend ETFs: Invest in exchange-traded funds that focus on high-dividend stocks.

72. Offer social media influencer management services: Help businesses collaborate with influencers to promote their products or services.

73. Start an online subscription box review blog: Review and promote subscription boxes on a blog and earn money through affiliate marketing.

74. Offer online accounting services: Help individuals or businesses manage their finances and bookkeeping remotely.

75. Become a virtual event host: Host virtual events or webinars for businesses and facilitate engaging discussions.

76. Offer personalized meal delivery services: Prepare and deliver customized meals to individuals or families.

77. Become a resume reviewer: Offer feedback and suggestions to individuals looking to improve their resumes.

78. Offer online marketing consulting services: Help businesses develop effective marketing strategies to reach their target audience.

79. Become a website tester: Test websites and provide feedback on user experience and functionality.

80. Offer online dance lessons: Teach others various dance styles through virtual lessons.

81. Become a social media manager for influencers: Help influencers manage their social media presence and partnerships.

82. Offer online personal styling services: Provide fashion advice and help individuals curate their wardrobes.

83. Become a cryptocurrency trader: Learn about cryptocurrency markets and trade digital currencies for profit.

84. Offer online interior design services: Help individuals or businesses design their spaces remotely.

85. Become a freelance copywriter: Write persuasive and compelling copy for businesses or individuals.

86. Offer online mindfulness or meditation classes: Guide individuals through mindfulness or meditation practices via video conferencing platforms.

87. Become an online dating consultant: Provide advice and assistance to individuals navigating the world of online dating.

88. Offer online business coaching: Help entrepreneurs and small business owners grow their businesses through coaching sessions.

89. Become a video editor: Edit videos for individuals or businesses who require professional-looking content.

90. Offer online personal training: Design workout programs and provide virtual training sessions to help individuals achieve their fitness goals.

91. Become a personal stylist: Help individuals develop their style and assist with shopping for clothing and accessories.